n and Wild

Vintage inspired gifts

Kerry Lucas

Worn and Wild by Kerry Lucas

First Published in Great Britain in 2019 by Beercott Books.

ISBN 978-1-9997429-3-5

Typesetting, photography, artwork and extra technical content by Simon Lucas

Any errors found after publication will be published on our website at beercottbooks.co.uk/errata

www.facebook.com/craftykestrel
www.craftykestrel.co.uk
www.beercottboooks.co.uk
www.facebook.com/beercottbooks
www.katiemcculloughphotography.co.uk

Beercott

Contents

Introduction

Welcome to my collection of vintage inspired gifts. In putting together this book I wanted to include a range of crafts, but I have stuck to those I know best - knitting, crochet and cooking. I have tried to keep the makes simple, but there are a couple of more advanced projects for those who like a challenge or would like to try new techniques.

Why Worn and Wild? Well the worn comes from the makes to wear, and the wild comes from references to animals, nature and the countryside.

I am a big lover of crafting, I find it very therapeutic. A great way to unwind as every day life seems to pass by at an ever-increasing pace. Creating things by hand also has the advantage that you get to choose where the ingredients or materials come from. I am a great believer in using natural resources, so you will find all the yarn I have used is either pure wool or cotton. While these materials can often be more expensive to purchase, they generally wear better, look better, and have less of an impact on the environment.

Each project is inspired either by a memory from my childhood such as baking with my nan and listening to her stories about a time when everyone used to make things at home through necessity, or simply a time when making things by hand was the pastime of choice!

Whatever you choose to make, enjoy the process as I am sure your friends and family will enjoy receiving the finished gifts.

Kerry

TOOLS AND MATERIALS

To complete all the projects in this book you will need the following:

3mm knitting needles

3mm double ended knitting needles

4mm knitting needles

4mm double ended knitting needles

4mm circular knitting needle

6mm knitting needles

3mm crochet hook

4mm crochet hook

5mm crochet hook

6mm safety eyes

7.5mm safety eyes

Embroidery thread

Toy stuffing

Quiltng cotton

Embroidery needle

Doll needle or sewing needle

Stitch holders

Stitch markers

DK wool in various colours - I have used both Drops LIMA (65% wool, 35% Alpaca) and Tofts DK (100% wool)

Super Chunky wool for felting in various colours - I have used Drops Eskimo (100% wool)

Aran weight cotton - I have used Drops Paris (100% cotton)

Spring

Tank Top
Crocheted Scrubbies
Little Chick
Lavender Mice
Easter Rocky Road

TANK TOP

This delightful pattern is very reminiscent of knits from the 1940's. It is worked in the round starting from the bottom rib. The neck and armhole rib are then worked by picking up stitches around the openings.

While more of a challenging knit, the extra effort will be well worth it.

MATERIALS

100g Toft DK in Lime Green (G)
100g Toft DK in Cream (C)
4mm circular needle or 4mm double pointed needles
embroidery needle.
Stitch markers
Stitch holders

Abbreviations: see page 115
Gauge: 22st and 31 rows to 10cm in stst.

Finished size: 54cm around the chest, 28cm from neck to bottom edge, 15.5cm from underarm to bottom edge.

MAIN BODY

Start by casting on 121 st in G. Join into a round making sure the stitches are not twisted, by slipping the first st from the the RIGHT needle to the LEFT needle, then k2tog (120 st).

Place a stitch marker here to mark the start of the rounds.

Round 1-6: (k2, p2) to end
Round 7-12: change to C and knit
Round 13-18: change to G and knit

Repeat rounds 7-18 until the work measures 13cm from the cast-on edge. Keeping the stripes correct, split the next round to form the back and front sections as follows:

Split round: cast off 6, k48, cast off 12, k48, cast of 6. Break yarn and fasten off.

The front sections and back are now worked separately on these groups of stitches.

BACK

Working on one set of 48st, rejoin yarn on the ws of the work and p48, turn. Continue to work in rows as follows:

Row 1: k2, skpo, k to last 4 st, k2tog, k2
Row 2: purl

repeat rows 1 & 2 three times, finishing on a purl row (40st)

Continue working in rows in stst keeping the colour stripes correct, until the armhole section measures 12cm (25cm overall). Place these 40st on a stitch holder.

FRONT

Working on the second set of 48st and with the WS facing, rejoin yarn keeping the stripes correct, p48, turn. Continue working in rows as follows:

Right Front shaping:

Row 1: k2, skpo, k 15, k2tog, k2, turn
Row 2: purl
Row 3: k2, skpo, k to last 4 st, k2tog, k2
Row 4: purl

repeat rows 3 & 4 until 15st remain, finishing with a purl row.

Row 5: k to last 4 st, k2tog, k2
Row 6: purl
repeat rows 5 & 6 until 10 st left.

Keep working in stst on these 10 st, keeping the stripes correct, until the front measures the same length as the back. Place these stitches on a stitch holder.

Left Front shaping:

Slip the next 2 stitches onto a stitch holder.

Rejoin yarn with RS facing and keeping the stripes correct, work in rows as follows:

Row 1: k2, skpo, k to last 4 st, k2tog, k2
Row 2: purl

repeat rows 1 & 2 until 15 st remain.

Row 3: k2, skpo, k to end
Row 4: purl

repeat rows 3 & 4 until 10 st left.

Keep working in stst on these 10 st, keeping the stripes correct, until the front measures the same length as the back. Place these stitches on a stitch holder.

Turn the tank top inside out. With RS together, join across the shoulders (10 st each shoulder) using the three needle cast-off method (see page 125). Turn the top RS out to work on the neck and shoulder bands.

NECK BAND

Using G, with RS facing, pick up 33 st down right front neck edge, k1 from the stitch holder at centre front, now place a st marker. Knit the remaining st from the stitch holder, then pick up 33 st up the left front. Finish the round by knitting across the 20 stitches of the back from the stitch holder. Now continue in rounds as follows:

Round 1: (k2, p2) to end
Round 2: work k2 p2 rib until you reach 2st from the stitch marker, k2tog, move marker to the right needle, skpo, then continue in k2 p2 rib to the end of the round.
Round 3: work k2 p2 rib until you reach 1 st from the stitch marker, p1, move marker to right needle, p1, then continue in k2 p2 rib to the end of the round.
Round 4: rpt round 2
Round 5: rpt round 3

Cast off in rib, making sure you decrease either side of the stitch marker as in round 2.

SHOULDER BANDS - work both armholes the same

Using G, pick up 64 st evenly around the armhole, starting at the centre of the underarm.

Work 5 rounds of k2 p2 rib.

Cast off in rib.

To finish off, sew in all loose ends.

Tip!
you could make a plain version by using a single colour
instead of the stripes.

CROCHETED SCRUBBIES

These simple to make scrubbies are ideal for removing make-up and applying other facial products. Made from 100% cotton yarn, they are easy to wash and re-use time and time again. Looked after properly, they should last for ages! They are also economical to make, as you can get 5 scrubbies from a single 50g ball of cotton.

MATERIALS:

Drops paris cotton in chosen colour
4mm crochet hook

PATTERN:

Round 1: Start by making a magic loop, ch 2 (counts as 1st tr), 12 tr into loop, join with ss

Round 2: 2 chain, tr into same space, 2tr into each st to end of round, join with ss

Round 3: 1ch, htr into same space, 2 htr into each st to end of round, join with ss and fasten off.

Sew in loose ends.

And that's it. They really are simple.

LITTLE CHICK

When I remember Easter as a child, I think of three things: little chicks, Easter eggs and rabbits. As I already have a rabbit pattern in my first book 'A Year in Woolly Wonders', I thought it would be fun to have a go at creating a little Easter chick. This is a very simple pattern and quick to make, but great fun.

MATERIALS.

Toft DK wool in camel
Toft DK wool in fudge
Toft DK wool in yellow
2 x 6mm safety eyes
stuffing
3mm knitting needles
3mm double ended needles
embroidery needle

HEAD

Starting at base, cast on 6 st in CAMEL

Row 1: (inc-kw) 6 times (12)
Row 2: purl
Row 3: (k1, inc-kw) 6 times (18)
Row 4: purl
Row 5: (k2, inc-kw) 6 times (24)
Row 6: purl
Row 7: (k3, inc-kw) 6 times (30)
Row 8: purl
Row 9: knit
Row 10: purl
Row 11: (k3, k2tog) 6 times (24)
Row 12: purl
Row 13: (k2, k2tog) 6 times (18)
Row 14: purl
Row 15: (k1, k2tog) 6 times (12)
Row 16: purl
Row 17: (k2tog) 6 times (6)

Break off yarn leaving a long end and transfer to a stitch holder.

Body

Starting at bottom Cast on 6 st in CAMEL

Row 1: (inc-kw) 6 times (12)
Row 2: purl
Row 3: (k1, inc-kw) 6 times (18)
Row 4: purl
Row 5: (k2, inc-kw) 6 times (24)
Row 6: purl
Row 7: (k3, inc-kw) 6 times (30)
Row 8: purl
Row 9: (k4, inc-kw) 6 times (36)
Row 10: purl
Row 11: (k5, inc-kw) 6 times (42)
Row 12-18: continue in stst starting and ending with a purl row.
Row 19: (k5, k2tog) 6 times (36)
Row 20: purl
Row 21: (k4, k2tog) 6 times (30)
Row 22: purl
Row 23: (k3, k2tog) 6 times (24)
Row 24: purl
Row 25: (k2, k2tog) 6 times (18)
Row 26: purl
Row 27: (k1, k2tog) 6 times (12)
Row 28: purl
Row 29: (k2tog) 6 times (6)

Break off yarn leaving a long end and transfer to a stitch holder.

Legs (make 2)

Using 3mm double-ended needles and leaving a long end, cast on 4 st in YELLOW and work i-cord as follows

Row 1: k4
Row 2: without turning the work, move the stitches to the other end of the needle, pass the wool round the back of the work. Keeping yarn tight, k4

Repeat row 2 until the leg measures 55mm.

Claws: continue in YELLOW

Row 1: inc-kw

Put the remaining stitches on a stitch holder, then continue working on these 2 stitches as for the leg, working 4 rows in total.
Cast off kw. Break yarn leaving an end.

Re-join yarn and work the same on the next 2 stitches for a total of 4 rows.
Cast off kw. Break yarn leaving an end.
Rejoin yarn into last st and inc-kw.
Work 4 rows in total on these 2 stitches.
Cast-off kw leaving an end.

Wings (Make 2)

Using CAMEL and 3mm needles cast on 3 st.

Row 1: inc-kw, k2 (4)
Row 2: knit

Row 3: inc-kw, k3 (5)
Row 4: knit
Row 5: knit
Row 6: knit
Row 7: inc-kw, k4 (6)
Row 8: knit
Row 9: knit
Row 10: knit
Row 11: inc-kw, k5 (7)
Row 12: k6, inc-kw (8)
Row 13: inc-kw, k7 (9)
Row 14: k8, inc-kw (10)
Row 15: inc-kw, k9 (11)
Row 16: knit
Row 17: k2tog, k7, k2tog (9)
Row 18: k2tog, k5, k2tog (7)
Row 19: k2tog, k3, k2tog (5)
Row 20: k2tog, k1, k2tog (3)
cast off kw. Break yarn leaving an
end for sewing the wing to the body.

BEAK

Using FUDGE and 3mm needles cast on 8
st

Row 1: knit
Row 2: k2tog, k4, k2tog (6)
Row 3: knit
Row 4: k2tog, k2, k2tog (4)
Row 5: knit
Row 6: k2tog twice (2)
Row 7: k2tog
Fasten off the yarn leaving an end to
sew beak together.

TO MAKE UP

HEAD

Fit the safety eyes roughly in the
middle of the head, and close
together. Thread the yarn from the
last row of the head through the
stitches remaining on the needle and
pull tight, then remove the stitches
from the needle. With right-sides
together, sew along the back of the
head, leaving a small gap at the base
for stuffing. Turn the head the right
way out, and stuff to the required
firmness. Sew together the remaining
opening and feed the end of the yarn
back through the head before cutting
off. Feed the remaining end back
through the head before cutting off.

BODY

Thread the yarn from the last row of
the body through the stitches
remaining on the needle and pull
tight, then remove the stitches from
the needle. With right-sides
together, sew along the back of the
body, leaving a small gap at the
bottom for stuffing. Turn the body
the right way out, and stuff to the
required firmness. Sew together the
remaining opening and feed the end of
the yarn back through the body before
cutting off. Feed the remaining end
back through the body before cutting
off.

LEGS

Thread the yarn from the last row of each claw back through the claw and cut. fasten off the threads at the base of each claw, and then feed the ends up the leg before trimming.

BEAK

Fold the beak in half and sew together along the edge to form a triangle, leaving the cast-on edge open. Feed the thread back through the beak before trimming.

ASSEMBLY:

Attach the head to the body, making sure the nose points forward (the body seam should be at the back).

Sew the beak to the front of the head, adding a little stuffing if desired.

Using the free thread, sew the wings to the sides of the body in the position shown.

Using the free thread, attach the legs to the underside of the body.

Lavender mice

My nan always used to tell me about lavender being used to keep away the moths and keep your clothes smelling fresh. These lavender mice are very quick and easy to make, and are great fun for hiding in your drawers! They have no eyes, but if you want to embroider them on or use a couple of black beads they would be very cute.

Materials:

50g Toft DK in Steel
25g Toft DK in Pink
3mm crochet hook
Toy stuffing
Embroidery needle
Lavender (optional)

Note you will be able to make several mice from this amount of yarn.

Main Body:

Using STEEL and a 3mm crochet hook, ch2.

Round 1: 3 DC into first ch.
Round 2: 2DC into each st (6)
Round 3: DC2, (2DC into next st) 4 times (10)
Round 4: DC 10
Round 5: DC3, 2DC into next st, DC, (2DC into next st) twice, DC, 2DC into next st, DC (14)
Round 6: DC 14
Round 7: DC 14

Round 8: DC3, 2DC into next st, DC, 2DC into next st, DTR3tog into the next st, DC2, DTR3tog into the next st, 2DC into next st, DC, 2DC into next st, DC (18)
Round 9: DC 18
Round 10: DC 18
Round 11: DC 18
Round 12: DC 18
Round 13: DC 2, (DC2tog, DC) twice, DC2tog (twice), (DC, DC2tog) twice (12)
Round 14: DC 12
Round 15: (DC2tog) 6 times (6)
Break off the yarn leaving a long end and fasten off.

Stuff the body, adding some lavender if desired, then gather the open end and fasten off. Sew in all loose ends.

Tail:

Using PINK and a 3mm crochet hook, pick up and chain 22. Sew in the loose ends.

Easter Rocky Road

This gloriously chocolatey treat is full of all the things that I used to love about Easter as a child. Chocolate, chocolate and more chocolate! It is very simple and quick to make, and doesn't usually last very long in our house.

Ingredients:

220g Milk chocolate
150g Extra dark chocolate
135g White chocolate
100g Golden syrup
100g Unsalted butter
100g Mini marshmallows
100g Shortbread biscuits chopped into small chunks
500g Easter chocolates

Method:

Place the milk chocolate and dark chocolate into a bowl together with the butter and golden syrup. Heat this gently either over a pan of gently boiling water or in short bursts in the microwave until the chocolate and butter have melted, stirring to make a smooth mixture.

Next add the chopped shortbread, marshmallows and half the Easter chocolates, stirring to make sure everything is coated in the chocolate and well mixed.

Line a 20cm square tin with baking parchment and pour the mixture into the tin. Level off gently.
Melt the white chocolate and gently pour over the top of the rocky road mixture, making sure you cover the entire surface.

Place the rest of the Easter chocolates over the top and press them gently into the white chocolate. Place the tin into the fridge and chill for around 2 hours until set and firm.

Remove from the tin, chop into chunks and enjoy.

Summer

Crocheted Strawberry
Beggars Shortbread
Felted Elephant
Royal Guardsman
Crocheted Bumble Bee

CROCHETED STRAWBERRY

This cute little strawberry is worked in rounds using the amigurumi method for the main section, while the calyx is worked in a combination of chain and double crochet. It is very quick to make so you could knock up a whole bowl full in no time.

MATERIALS

Scraps of Drops Lima DK wool in red and green
Small amount of yellow embroidery thread
Stuffing
Embroidery needle
3mm crochet hook.

MAIN BODY

Using RED, start by making a magic ring, and dc x 6 into the ring.
Round 2: dc into each st
Round 3: (2dc, dc) 3 times (9)
Round 4: dc into each st
Round 5: (2dc, dc, dc) 3 times (12)
Round 6: dc into each st
Round 7: (2dc, dc) 6 times (18)
Round 8 & 9: dc into each st
Round 10: (dc2tog, dc) 6 times (12)
Round 11: (dc2tog) 6 times (6)

Fasten off then stuff. Close the open end by gathering through the stitches, pulling tight and fasten off.

CALYX

*Using GREEN, ch 4
dc into second chain from hook.
dc into each remaining chain*
Repeat from * to * 3 times

join to first chain using a slip stitch and fasten off.

Attach the calyx to the top of the strawberry, and sew in all loose ends.

Using a small amount of yellow embroidery thread, make small stitches in a random pattern over the strawberry.

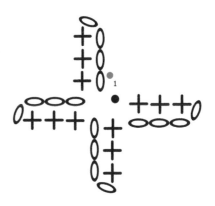

Calyx stitch chart

Beggars shortbread

My grandad loved biscuits, so I could not write a book of memories and gifting without some shortbread for Grandad Stan.

Ingredients

200g plain flour
100g rice flour
200g butter
100g caster sugar
200g dark chocolate
25cm loose-bottom round cake tin

Method

Heat oven to 160°C (fan).

Prepare the cake tin by lining the base with baking paper / parchment.

Place the butter and sugar in a mixing bowl and mix until they form a smooth creamy mixture.

Sift in the plain four and rice flour and mix together gently until the mixture starts to come together and looks like breadcrumbs.

Press the mixture into the prepared tin and prick all over with a fork. I like to press the prongs of the fork around the edge to make a pattern, or you could pinch with your fingers.

Place the tin in the oven and cook for around 30 mins or until lightly golden and firm.

Leave to cool in the tin.

TOPPING.

Break the chocolate into pieces in a heat proof bowl, then place the bowl over a pan of gently boiling water. Stir the chocolate until it has all melted.

Remove from the heat and pour the chocolate over the shortbread, then allow to cool.

Chill in the fridge, then cut into shapes and enjoy!

Tip!
For a slightly richer alternative, replace half the butter with clotted cream.

Felted Elephant

This cute little fellow reminds me of an old circus illustration from the 1950's with his little striped hat and dungarees. As with the bear and panda which feature later in the book, he is created by knitting a simple pattern then using a hot felting process to produce the smooth, dense effect of the body, head, ears arms and legs. You can read how I do the felting process on page 122.

Materials:

100g of Drops Eskimo in your chosen colour (I like to use medium grey)
50g of Drops Lima DK wool in your chosen colour for the dungarees
Small amounts of drops Eskimo in each colour for the hat
Strong quilting cotton
Doll needle
4 small buttons
A pair of 7mm safety eyes
4mm knitting needles
6mm knitting needles
6mm crochet hook

Body

Using 6mm needles and Drops Eskimo, work the standard body from page 119.

With RS together, feed the yarn through the remaining stitches, remove them from the needle and pull tight. Sew along the outer edges of the body, leaving a small opening near the bottom.

Turn the body right side out, and stuff lightly before closing the opening and fastening off the end of the yarn. Feed the remaining end back through the body and cut off the excess.

HEAD

Using 6mm needles and Drops Eskimo,
cast on 3 st

Row 1: inc-kw 3 times (6)
Row 2: purl
Row 3-14: starting with a knit row,
continue in stst

Now continue with the standard head
from row 3 onwards.

Break yarn leaving a long end for
sewing up the head.

Feed the yarn through the remaining
stitches, remove them from the needle
and pull tight.

Fix the safety eyes using the picture
opposite as a guide. Bear in mind
that the head will shrink during the
felting process.

Placing WS together, sew along the
outer edges of the head and along the
trunk using mattress stitch, stuffing
lightly as you go.

Cloee the opening and fastening off
the end of the yarn.

Feed the remaining end back through
thetk and cut off the excess.

ARMS / LEGS

Using 6mm needles and Drops Eskimo
work the standard arms and legs from
page 119.

With RS together, feed the yarn
through the remaining stitches,
remove them from the needle and pull
tight. Sew along the outer edges of
the arm / leg, leaving a small
opening near the bottom.

Turn the body right side out, and
stuff lightly before closing the
opening and fastening off the end of
the yarn. Feed the remaining end back
through the arm / leg and cut off the
excess.

EARS - make 2

Cast on 4st
Row 1: inc-kw, k2, inc-kw (6)
Row 2: inc-kw, k4, inc-kw (8)
Row 3: inc-kw, k6, inc-kw (10)
Row 4: inc-kw, k8, inc-kw (12)
Row 5: inc-kw, k10, inc-kw (14
Row 6: inc-kw, k12, inc-kw (16)
Row 7-10: knit
Row 11: cast off 8, k7 (8)
Row 12-13: knit
Row 14: k6, k2tog (7)
Cast off.

Attach the ears to the sides of the
head, using the picture as a guide.

Now it is time for the felting
process. For detailed instructions of

the method I use, refer to page 122.
Sometimes you can be left with small
holes in the felted surface, where
the stuffing can poke through. If
these are not too large, they can
either be darned, or alternatively
you could cover them by sewing a
small patch of colourful fabric over
the opening. Sometime though there is
no option but to re-make the piece.

Once you are happy all the pieces
have felted correctly, you can
proceed to assemble the elephant.

Attach the head, arms and legs to the
body using a strong cotton. I like to
use quilting thread as it is
extremely strong. Be careful when
pulling it tight though - I have been
known to cut myself with the thread!
I also like to use a doll needle.
These are essentially very long
needles, and make reaching under the
head much easier. If you don't have
these then a normal sewing needle
will do.

THE DUNGAREES.

The dungarees are worked flat by
knitting two legs, then knitting
across both to form the body.

Using 4mm needles and your chosen
colour in Drops Lima, cast on 26st
for the first leg.

Work 6 rows in stst starting with a
knit row, then break off the yarn,
and leave these stitches on the LEFT
needle.

Cast on another 26st for the second
leg, making sure the stitches are on
the same needle as the first leg (the
RS of the first leg should be facing
you).

Work 6 rows in stst.

You now work the body as follows:

Row 1: k26 across the second leg,
then k26 across the first leg (52)
Row 2: purl
Row 3-16: continue is stst, starting
with a knit row.

Cast off, leaving a long thread for
sewing up.

STRAPS - make 2

Using 4mm needles and your chosen
colour of Drops Lima, cast on 4st.

Knit 76 rows and cast off.

Sew in all loose ends.

Making up the dungarees

Fold one leg in half with RS facing, and sew up the leg to the crotch.

Fold the second leg in half with RS facing and sew up to the crotch, now continue to join the back seam of the main body of the dungarees, then turn RS out. Sew in all loose ends.

Attach one end of a strap to the back of the dungarees, placing the strap approximately 4 stitches away from the centre seam. Repeat with the other strap.

Now fasten the other ends of the straps to the front of the dungarees, making sure they cross over. They should be approximately 6 stitches each side of centre.

Fix a button to each strap where they join the dungarees.

Circus hat.

The circus hat is crocheted rather than knitted, and is then felted like the elephant. It is worked in continuous rounds using the amigurumi method.

Using a 6mm crochet hook and colour A, make a magic ring.

Round 1: 6dc into a magic ring.
Round 2: dc into each stitch
Round 3: (dc, 2dc into next st) 3 times (9)
Round 4: dc into each st
Round 5: change to colour B, (2dc, 2dc into next st) 3 times (12)
Round 6: dc into each st
Round 7: (3dc, 2dc into next st) 3 times (15)
Round 8: dc into each st
Round 9: change to colour A, (4dc, 2dc into next stitch) 3 times (18)
Round 10: dc into each st
Round 11: (5dc, 2dc into next st) 3 times (21)
Round 12: dc into each st.

Join back to the previous round using
a ss and fasten off.

Sew in any loose ends, then felt.

Attach to the elephants head, between
the ears, but pointing backwards.

Royal Guardsman

No vintage handmade book would be complete without the iconic British soldier. Dressed in traditional red, black and gold he looks very smart and ready for duty at Buckingham Palace.

Materials.

DK wool in yellow
DK wool in black
DK wool in pink
DK wool in red
stuffing
3mm knitting needles
3mm double ended needles
4mm knitting needles
embroidery needle

Head

Starting at base, using 3mm needles cast on 6 st in PINK

Row 1: (inc-kw) 6 times (12)
Row 2: purl
Row 3: (k1, inc-kw) 6 times (18)
Row 4: purl
Row 5: (k2, inc-kw) 6 times (24)
Row 6: purl
Row 7: (k3, inc-kw) 6 times (30)
Row 8: purl
Row 9: knit
Row 10: purl
Row 11: (k3, k2tog) 6 times (24)
Row 12: purl
Row 13: (k2, k2tog) 6 times (18)
Row 14: purl
Row 15: (k1, k2tog) 6 times (12)
Row 16: purl
Row 17: (k2tog) 6 times (6)

Break off yarn leaving a long end and transfer to a stitch holder.

Body.

Starting at the base of the body using 3mm needles cast on 6 st in BLACK

Row 1: (inc-kw) 6 times (12)
Row 2: purl
Row 3: (k1, inc-kw) 6 times (18)
Row 4: purl
Row 5: (k2, inc-kw) 6 times (24)
Row 6: purl
Row 7: k10, inc-kw, k2, inc-kw, k10 (26)
Row 8: p10, inc-pw, p1, inc-pw twice, p1, inc-pw, p10 (30)
Row 9: k10, inc-kw, k1, inc-kw, k4, inc-kw, k1, inc-kw, k10 (34)
Row 10: purl
Row 11: knit
Row 12: change to RED, purl
Row 13: k10, k2tog, k1, k2tog, k4, k2tog, k1, k2tog, k10 (30)
Row 14: p10, p2tog, p1, p2tog twice, p1, p2tog, p10 (26)
Row 15: k10, k2tog, k2, k2tog, k10 (24)
Row 16-26: continue in stst starting and ending with a purl row
Row 27: (k2, k2tog) 6 times (18)
Row 28: purl
Row 29: (k1, k2tog) 6 times (12)
Row 30: purl
Row 31: (k2tog) 6 times (6)

Break off yarn leaving a long end to sew up body, and transfer stitches to a stitch holder.

Arms (make 2)

Using 3mm double-ended needles and leaving a long end, cast on 3 st using WHITE and work 6 rows of i-cord as follows

Row 1: k3
Row 2: Without turning the work, move the stitches to the other end of the needle, pass the wool round the back of the work. Keeping yarn tight, k3
Row 3-6: Repeat row 2

Now change to RED and continue working i-cord until the arm measures 85mm

Break off yarn leaving a long end, and transfer stitches to a stitch holder.

Legs (make 2)

Using 3mm double-ended needles and leaving a long end, cast on 4 st using BLACK and work i-cord as follows

Row 1: k4
Row 2: without turning the work, move the stitches to the other end of the needle, pass the wool round the back of the work. Keeping yarn tight, k4.

Repeat row 2 until the leg measures 95mm.

Break off yarn leaving a long end, and transfer stitches to a stitch holder

Boots (make 2)

Using BLACK and 4mm needles cast on 14 st

Row 1-2: knit
Row 3: K3, (K2tog) 4 times, K3 (10)
Row 4: K3, (K2tog) twice, K3 (8)
Row 5-6: knit
Cast-off knit-wise.

Break off yarn leaving a long end.

Hat

Using BLACK and 3mm needles cast on 26 st

Row 1-16: work in stst, starting with a knit row
Row 17: (k2tog) 13 times (13)
Row 18: purl
Row 19: (k2tog) 6 times, k1 (7)

Break off yarn leaving a long end, and transfer stitches to a stitch holder

Chin Strap

Using 3mm double-ended needles and leaving a long end, cast on 2 st using YELLOW and work i-cord as follows

Row 1: k2
Row 2: Without turning the work, move the stitches to the other end of the needle, pass the wool round the back of the work. Keeping yarn tight, k2. Repeat row 2 until the strap is long enough to reach from one side of the hat, under his chin to the other side of his hat (approximately 55 mm).

Break off yarn leaving a long end, and transfer stitches to a stitch holder

To make up

Head

Thread the yarn from the last row of the head through the stitches remaining on the needle and pull tight, then remove the stitches from the needle. With right-sides together, sew along the back of the head, leaving a small gap at the base for stuffing. Turn the head the right way out, and stuff to the required firmness. Sew together the remaining opening and feed the end of the yarn back through the head before cutting off. Feed the remaining end back through the head before cutting off.

Body

Thread the yarn from the last row of the body through the stitches remaining on the needle and pull tight, then remove the stitches from the needle. With right-sides together, sew along the back of the body, leaving a small gap at the bottom for stuffing. Turn the body the right way out, and stuff to the required firmness. Sew together the remaining opening and feed the end of the yarn back through the body before cutting off. Feed the remaining end back through the body before cutting off.

BOOTS

Fold the boot in half and stitch down the back and along the bottom of the boot.

ARMS

Thread the yarn from the last row of the arm through the stitches remaining on the needle and pull tight, then remove the stitches from the needle. Fasten off this end securely. Weave the other loose end up through the arm and cut off the excess.

LEGS

Thread the yarn from the last row of the leg through the stitches remaining on the needle and pull tight, then remove the stitches from the needle.

Fasten off this end securely. Weave the other loose end up through the leg and cut off the excess.

HAT

Thread the yarn from the last row of the hat through the stitches remaining on the needle and pull tight, then remove the stitches from the needle.

With right-sides together, sew along the back of the hat. Feed the remaining end back through the hat before cutting off.

CHIN STRAP

Thread the yarn from the last row of the strap through the stitches remaining on the needle and pull tight, then remove the stitches from the needle. Fasten off this end securely.

ASSEMBLY:

Attach the head to the body, making sure both seams are at the back.

Using the free thread, attach the arms to the body just below the head, one on each side.

Using the free thread, attach the legs to the underside of the body. Feed each leg into a boot and fasten with a small stitch.

Using some black wool, sew a small moustache onto the front of the face just below half way up.

Using some yellow wool, make some small stitches to represent his buttons.

Stuff the hat lightly and attach to the head. It should come down to just above the moustache at the front, and tip backwards slightly, fitting lower at the back.

Attach the chin strap at either side of the head, just under the edge of the hat so that it passes under the guardsman's chin.

CROCHET BUMBLE BEE

I am lucky enough to have a traditional cottage garden and I enjoy supporting the British bee. Did you know there are over 24 species of bumble bee in Britain?

This little crocheted bee is very simple and quick to make from scraps of yarn, and could be made into a variety of things.

I used Drops Lima in black, white and goldenrod, but any DK wool would be fine.

MATERIALS

Scraps of DK yarn in black, white & yellow
4mm crochet hook
Stuffing

BODY

The body is worked in continuous rounds.

Using black, dc 6 into a magic ring
Round 1: 2dc into each stitch (12)
Round 2 & 3: change to yellow and work 2 rounds of dc into each st
Round 4 & 5: change to black and work 2 rounds of dc into each st
Round 6 & 7: change to yellow and work 2 rounds of dc into each st
Round 8 & 9: change to black and work 2 rounds of dc into each st
Round 10: 2dctog 6 times (6)

Fasten off yarn, stuff the body then gather stitches together to close off the opening at the head end of the body and fasten off the end.

WINGS (MAKE 2)

Using white, chain 6
dc into second chain from hook
tr, dtr into same stitch
dtr, tr, dc into next stitch
dc into next stitch
dc, tr, dtr, ttr into next stitch
ttr, dtr, tr, dc into next stitch
fasten off.

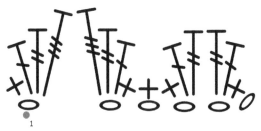

Bee wing stitch chart

MAKING UP

Place the wings together and sew along the foundation chain edge.
Open out the wings, then sew to the body. The larger wing section should be pointing to the head end of the body.
Sew in all loose ends.

Autumn

Harvest Wreath
Nan's Hedgerow Jam
Apple Pincushion
Felted Bear
Fingerless Gloves
Willow the Witch

HARVEST WREATH

The woodland and countryside are very close to my heart so in this chapter of harvest and Autumn I had to include leaves in oranges and browns.

MATERIALS.

Wreath made from twigs, available from craft shops or the internet. The one I used was about 20cm in diameter.
DK wool in autumn colours for the leaves
DK wool in yellow or orange for the pumpkin, and brown for the stalk.
4mm knitting needles
3mm double-ended knitting needles
embroidery needle
stuffing

AUTUMN LEAF

STALK

Using 3mm double ended needles cast on 3 st.

Work i-cord as follows:
Row 1: k3
Row 2: without turning the work, move the stitches to the other end of the needle, pass the wool round the back of the work. Keeping yarn tight, k3

Repeat row 2 until the stalk measures approximately 2.5 cm

Main Leaf

Continue for the main leaf as follows:

Row 1: k1, p1, k1
Row 2: inc-pw, k1, inc-pw (5)
Row 3: (inc-kw) twice, p1, (inc-kw) twice (9)
Row 4: p4, k, p4
Row 5: (k1, inc-kw) twice, p1, (inc-kw, k1) twice (13)
Row 6: p6, k1, p6
Row 7: (k1, inc-kw) 3 times, p1, (inc-kw, k1) 3 times (19)
Row 8: p9, k1, p9
Row 9: cast off 4 kw, k4, p1, k9 (15)
Row 10: cast off 4 pw, p4, k1, p5 (11)
Row 11: k1, inc-kw, k2, inc-kw, p1, inc-kw, k2, inc-kw, k1 (15)
Row 12: p1, (inc-pw, p2) twice, k1, (p2, inc-pw) twice, p1 (19)
Row 13: cast off 5 kw, k3, p1, k9 (14)
Row 14: cast off 5 pw, p3, k1, p4 (9)
Row 15: (k1, inc-kw) twice, p1, (inc-kw, kw) twice (13)
Row 16: p6, k1, p6
Row 17: k2, inc-kw, k3, p1, k3, inc-kw, k2 (15)
Row 18: p7, k1, p7
Row 19: cast off 4 kw, k2, p1, k7 (11)
Row 20: cast off 4 pw, p2, k1, p3 (7)
Row 21: k2tog, k1, p1, k1, k2tog (5)
Row 22: p2tog, k1, p2tog (3)
Row 23: k3
Row 24: p3
Row 25: k3tog (1)

Break yarn and fasten off. Sew in all loose ends.

Pumpkin

Pumpkin

Starting at bottom Cast on 6 st in YELLOW / ORANGE using 4mm needles

Row 1: inc-kw 6 times (12)
Row 2: knit
Row 3: (k1, inc-kw) 6 times (18)
Row 4: knit
Row 5: (k2, inc-kw) 6 times (24)
Row 6: knit
Row 7: (k3, inc-kw) 6 times (30)
Row 8: knit
Row 9: (k4, inc-kw) 6 times (36)
Row 10: knit
Row 11: (k5, inc-kw) 6 times (42)
Row 12-16: knit
Row 17: (k5, k2tog) 6 times (36)
Row 18: knit
Row 19: (k4, k2tog) 6 times (30)
Row 20: knit
Row 21: (k3, k2tog) 6 times (24)
Row 22: knit
Row 23: (k2, k2tog) 6 times (18)
Row 24: knit
Row 25: (k1, k2tog) 6 times (12)
Row 26: knit
Row 27: k2tog 6 times (6)

Break off yarn leaving a long end and transfer to a stitch holder.

Stalk

Using 3mm double-ended needles and leaving a long end, cast on 3 st

using BROWN and work i-cord as follows

Row 1: k3
Row 2: without turning the work, move the stitches to the other end of the needle, pass the wool round the back of the work. Keeping yarn tight, k3

Repeat row 2 until the stalk measures 2cm.

Break off yarn leaving a long end, and transfer stitches to a stitch holder.

ASSEMBLY

Thread the yarn from the last row of the pumpkin through the stitches remaining on the needle and pull tight, then remove the stitches from the needle.

With right-sides together, sew along the back of the pumpkin, leaving a small gap at the bottom for stuffing.

Turn the pumpkin the right way out, and stuff to the required firmness. Sew together the remaining opening and fasten off without breaking the yarn. Now feed the yarn through the pumpkin from the bottom to the top and then back again. Pull on the yarn to make a dimple in the top of the pumpkin, then fasten off the thread. Feed the end back through the pumpkin, then around the outside, and then back through the pumpkin and pull to create the first ridge on the outside.

Repeat this 4 more times before fastening off the thread. Pass the thread back through the pumpkin before cutting off. Feed the remaining loose end back through the body before cutting off.

Thread the yarn from the last row of the stalk through the stitches remaining on the needle and pull tight, then remove the stitches from the needle. Fasten off this end securely. Weave the other loose end up through the stalk and cut off the excess.

Attach the stalk in the centre of the dimple in the top of the pumpkin and fasten off. Thread the loose end back through the pumpkin before cutting off.

ASSEMBLING THE WREATH

Once you have enough leaves and pumpkins, it is time to assemble the wreath. There is no hard and fast design here. How many leaves and pumpkins you require will depend on the size of wreath you have purchased.

Arrange the pumpkins and leaves around the wreath until you are happy with the layout. Start by attaching the pumpkins to the wreath using either some strong thread or matching yarn. I used a long doll needle to allow me to feed the thread through the twigs, but you could just tie the pumpkins on, or even use a hot glue gun.

Once the pumpkins are attached, start to fix the leaves in place in a similar manner.

When everything is attached, tie a piece of ribbon to the top of the wreath for hanging.

Nan's Hedgerow Jam

As a child I can remember my nan spending many hours making delicious jams and chutneys. Just thinking about the glorious smells makes me feel warm and cosy. One of my favourite pastimes in early autumn, is to go foraging for blackberries in the hedgerows. With this recipe I have combined the two, using foraged blackberries together with some apples from the tree in my garden.

There is no magic recipe for jam, but a rule of thumb is to use the same weight in sugar as you have in fruit, the other important ingredient being pectin to help it set. Different fruits contain different amounts of pectin, so adding something like apples or lemon juice can help with the setting process. You can also buy jam sugar which has added pectin, but I just use plain granulated sugar - it is often cheaper!

Ingredients

1kg blackberries
1kg granulated sugar
2 medium cooking apples
100ml water

several empty jam jars with lids
large saucepan

Method

Before you start making the jam, you will need to sterilise the jars. A very simple way to do this, is to give them a good wash in hot soapy water. Rinse them well with boiling water, then place on a baking tray. Place the jars in the oven at about 120°C for about 20 mins.

While the jars are in the oven you can make the jam. Wash the blackberries and remove any stalks before adding to a large saucepan. Peel and core the apples, chop into small chunks and add to the pan. Add the water and the sugar and give it a good stir.

Bring everything slowly to the boil on a medium heat, stirring all the time to ensure the sugar does not

burn. Once all the sugar has
dissolved, continue to boil the
mixture for about 15 mins, stirring
occasionally.

To test if the jam is ready, spoon a
small amount onto a cold saucer. If
you drag your finger lightly across
the surface of the jam and it
wrinkles, then the jam is ready. If
not, then simply boil the mixture for
another few minutes and try again.

Once the jam is ready, simply spoon
into the prepared jars and put the
lids on. As the jam cools it will
form a tight seal between the lid and
the jar.

APPLE PINCUSHION

Anyone who knows me, knows how much I enjoy eating natural foods. My favourite snack is an apple, and these are so fast to knit up they should become a favourite with you.

MATERIALS.

DK wool in green or red for apple, green for the leaves and brown for the stalk.
3mm knitting needles
3mm double-ended knitting needles
embroidery needle
stuffing

APPLE

Starting at bottom Cast on 6 st in GREEN / RED

Row 1: inc-kw 6 times (12)
Row 2: purl
Row 3: (k1, inc-kw) 6 times (18)
Row 4: purl
Row 5: (k2, inc-kw) 6 times (24)
Row 6: purl
Row 7: (k3, inc-kw) 6 times (30)
Row 8: purl
Row 9: (k4, inc-kw) 6 times (36)
Row 10: purl
Row 11: (k5, inc-kw) 6 times (42)
Row 12: purl
Row 13: knit
Row 14: purl
Row 15: knit
Row 16: purl
Row 17: (k5, k2tog) 6 times (36)
Row 18: purl
Row 19: (k4, k2tog) 6 times (30)
Row 20: purl
Row 21: (k3, k2tog) 6 times (24)
Row 22: purl
Row 23: (k2, k2tog) 6 times (18)
Row 24: purl
Row 25: (k1, k2tog) 6 times (12)
Row 26: purl
Row 27: k2tog 6 times (6)

Break off yarn leaving a long end and transfer to a stitch holder.

LEAF

Using GREEN cast on 2 st

Row 1: (inc-kw) twice (4)
Row 2: knit
Row 3: inc-kw, k2, inc-kw (6)
Row 4: knit
Row 5: k2tog, k2, k2tog (4)
Row 6: knit
Row 7: (k2tog) twice (2)
Row 8: knit
Row 9: k2tog (1)

Break off yarn, cast off and fasten off yarn.

STALK

Using 3mm double-ended needles and leaving a long end, cast on 3 st using BROWN and work i-cord as follows

Row 1: k3
Row 2: without turning the work, move the stitches to the other end of the needle, pass the wool round the back of the work. Keeping yarn tight, k3
Repeat row 2 until the stalk measures 2cm.

Break off yarn leaving a long end, and transfer stitches to a stitch holder.

ASSEMBLY

Thread the yarn from the last row of the apple through the stitches remaining on the needle and pull tight, then remove the stitches from the needle.

With right-sides together, sew along the back of the apple, leaving a small gap at the bottom for stuffing. Turn the apple the right way out, and stuff firmly.

Sew together the remaining opening and fasten off without breaking the yarn. Now feed the yarn through the apple from the bottom to the top and then back again. Pull on the yarn to create dimple in the top of the apple, then fasten off the thread.

Feed the end back through the apple before cutting off. Feed the remaining end back through the body before cutting off.

Thread the yarn from the last row of the stalk through the stitches remaining on the needle and pull tight, then remove the stitches from the needle. Fasten off this end securely. Weave the other loose end up through the stalk and cut off the excess.

Attach the stalk in the centre of the dip in the top of the apple and fasten off. Thread the loose end back through the apple before cutting off.

Thread the loose end from one end of the leaf back through the leaf before cutting off.

Attach the leaf to the apple as close to the bottom of the stalk as possible and fasten off. Thread the loose end back through the apple before cutting.

Felted Bear

This cute little felted bear is great fun to knit and will be treasured for years to come.

He is quick, easy to make and the Drops Eskimo felts up beautifully.

Materials

100g Drops Eskimo in your chosen colour
50g of Drops Lima DK wool in your chosen colour for the dungarees
4mm knitting needles
6mm knitting needles
1 pair 6.5mm safety eyes
toy stuffing
darning needle

Body

Using 6mm needles and Drops Eskimo, work the standard body from page 119.

With RS together, feed the yarn through the remaining stitches, remove them from the needle and pull tight. Sew along the outer edges of the body, leaving a small opening near the bottom.

Turn the body right side out, and stuff lightly before closing the opening and fastening off the end of the yarn. Feed the remaining end back through the body and cut off the excess.

Head

Using 6mm needles and Drops Eskimo, work the standard head from page 119.

Feed the yarn through the remaining stitches, remove them from the needle and pull tight. Fix the safety eyes using the picture as a guide. Bear in mind that the head will shrink during the felting process.

Placing RS together, sew along the outer edges of the head, leaving a small opening near the back of the head.

Turn the head right side out, and stuff lightly before closing the opening and fastening off the end of the yarn. Feed the remaining end back through the head and cut off the excess.

ARMS / LEGS

Using 6mm needles and Drops Eskimo, work the standard arms and legs from page 119.

With RS together, feed the yarn through the remaining stitches, remove them from the needle and pull tight. Sew along the outer edges of the arm / leg, leaving a small opening near the bottom.

Turn the body right side out, and stuff lightly before closing the opening and fastening off the end of the yarn. Feed the remaining end back through the arm / leg and cut off the excess.

EARS (make 2)

Using 6mm needles and Drops Eskimo, cast on 2st.

Row 1: (inc-kw) twice (4)
Row 2-5: knit
Row 6: (k2tog) twice (2)

Break off yarn leaving a long end.

Feed the yarn through the remaining stitches, remove them from the needle and pull tight. Fasten off the yarn and sew in the loose end.

Attach the ears to the sides of the head, using the picture as a guide.

FELTING

Now it is time for the felting process. For detailed instructions of the method I use, refer to page 122.

Sometimes you can be left with small holes in the felted surface, where the stuffing can poke through. If these are not too large, they can either be darned, or alternatively you could cover them by sewing a small patch of colourful fabric over the opening. Sometimes though there is no option but to re-make the piece.

Once you are happy all the pieces have felted correctly, you can proceed to assemble the bear. Attach the head, arms and legs to the body using a strong cotton. I like to use quilting thread as it is extremely strong. Be careful when pulling it tight though - I have been known to cut myself with the thread! I also like to use a doll needle. These are essentially very long needles, and make reaching under the head much easier. If you don't have these then a normal sewing needle will do.

Using some black embroidery thread, sew the nose and mouth as described on page 124.

The Dungarees.

The dungarees are worked flat by knitting two legs, then knitting across both to form the body.

Using 4mm needles and your chosen colour of drops Lima, cast on 26st for the first leg.

Work 6 rows in stst starting with a knit row.

Break off the yarn, and leave these stitches on the LEFT needle.

Cast on another 26st for the second leg, making sure the stitches are on the same needle as the first leg (the RS of the first leg should be facing you).

Work 6 rows in stst.

You now work the body as follows:

Row 1: k26 across the second leg, then k26 across the first leg (52)
Row 2: purl
Row 3-16: continue is stst, starting with a knit row.
Cast off, leaving a long thread for sewing up.

Straps - make 2

Using 4mm needles and your chosen colour of Drops Lima, cast on 4st. Knit 76 rows and cast off.

Making up the Dungarees

Fold one leg in half with RS facing, and sew up the leg to the crotch. Fold the second leg in half with RS facing and sew up to the crotch, now continue to join the back seam of the main body of the dungarees, then turn RS out. Sew in all loose ends.

Attach one end of a strap to the back of the dungarees, placing the strap approximately 4 stitches away from the centre seam. Repeat with the other strap.

Now fasten the other ends of the straps to the front of the dungarees, making sure they cross over. They should be approximately stitches each side of centre.

Fix a button to each strap where they join the dungarees.

Fingerless gloves

These lovely gloves are a perfect project for those autumn evenings. They can be made from a single ball of DK yarn. I used Drops Lima for these, but any good DK yarn would work well.

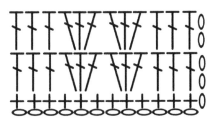

main pattern section
stitch chart

Materials
50g Drops Lima DK in Green Mix
5mm hook

Left Glove

Rib section (same for both gloves)

Chain 9
Row 1: dc into 2nd ch from hook then dc to end (8 DC) turn
Row 2: 1c, dc into back loop only of first dc, dc into back loop only of remaining dc (8 dc)
Row 3 - 24: rpt row 2
Fold in half and join into ring by ss through dc on first and last row 8 times (8ss)

Main section up to thumb hole - work in rounds, closing each round by ss into the start ch.

Row 1: 1ch, dc into each row of rib (24 dc)
Row 2: 2ch, tr into first st, 2tr, (miss next st, 3tr into the same st, miss next st) twice, 15 tr (24)
Row 3 - 5: rpt row 2
Row 6: 1ch, dc into first stitch then dc to end (24 dc).

THUMB HOLE - work in rows, turning after each row. Do NOT join into rounds!

Row 7: 2ch, tr into first st, 2tr, (miss next st, 3tr into the same st, miss next st) twice, 15 tr, TURN
Row 8: 2ch, tr into first st, 14tr, (miss next st, 3tr into the same st, miss next st) twice, 3 tr TURN
Row 9: 2ch, tr into first st, 2tr, (miss next st, 3tr into the same st, miss next st) twice, 15 tr, TURN
Row 10: 2ch, tr into first st, 14tr, (miss next st, 3tr into the same st, miss next st) twice, 3 tr TURN

FINGER SECTION - work in rounds, closing each round by ss into the start ch.

Row 11: 1ch, dc into first stitch then dc to end (24 dc), close round using ss
Row 12: 2ch, tr into first st, 2tr, (miss next st, 3tr into the same st, miss next st) twice, 15tr
Row 13-14: repeat row 12
Row 15: 1ch, dc into first stitch then dc to end (24 dc), close round then fasten off.

THUMB (same for both gloves) - work in rounds closing each round by ss into start ch

Row 1: starting at bottom of thumb opening, join thread then 1ch, 16 dc evenly spaced around opening (8 dc each side), close round
Row 2: 1ch, dc2tog, 12 dc, dc2tog, close round
Row 3: 1ch, dc2tog, 10 dc, dc2tog, close round
Row 4: 1ch, dc2tog, 8dc, dc2tog, close round and fasten off

Darn in loose ends.

RIGHT GLOVE

Work rib section from Left glove

MAIN SECTION UP TO THUMB HOLE - work in rounds, closing each round by ss into the start ch.

Row 1: 1ch, dc into each row of rib (24 dc)
Row 2: 2ch, tr into first st, 14tr, (miss next st, 3tr into the same st, miss next st) twice, 3 tr (24)
Row 3 - 5: rpt row 2
Row 6: 1ch, dc into first stitch then dc to end (24 dc).

THUMB HOLE - work in rows, turning after each row. Do NOT join into rounds!

Row 7: 2ch, tr into first st, 14tr,

(miss next st, 3tr into the same st, miss next st) twice, 3tr, TURN

Row 8: 2ch, tr into first st, 2tr, (miss next st, 3tr into the same st, miss next st) twice, 15tr, TURN

Row 9: 2ch, tr into first st, 14tr, (miss next st, 3tr into the same st, miss next st) twice, 3tr, TURN

Row 10: 2ch, tr into first st, 2tr, (miss next st, 3tr into the same st, miss next st) twice, 15tr, TURN

FINGER SECTION - work in rounds, closing each round by ss into the start ch.

Row 11: 1ch, dc into first stitch then dc to end (24 dc), close round using ss

Row 12: Row 2: 2ch, tr into first st, 14tr, (miss next st, 3tr into the same st, miss next st) twice, 3tr

Row 13 -14: rpt row 12

Row 15: 1ch, dc into first stitch then dc to end (24 dc), close round then fasten off.

Work thumb section from the Left glove.

Darn in loose ends.

Willow the Witch

I love Autumn as it is my birthday season. I made Willow as a fun knit for Halloween. She is quick and easy to knit, a great project for a beginner.

Materials:

25g Toft DK wool in lime green
50g Toft DK wook in black
25g Toft DK wool in steel
2 x 6mm black safety eyes
stuffing
3mm knitting needles
3mm double ended needles
4mm knitting needles
embroidery needle

Head

Starting at base, cast on 6 st in LIME GREEN

Row 1: (inc-kw) 6 times (12)
Row 2: purl
Row 3: (k1, inc-kw) 6 times (18)
Row 4: purl
Row 5: (k2, inc-kw) 6 times (24)
Row 6: purl
Row 7: (k3, inc-kw) 6 times (30)
Row 8: purl
Row 9: knit
Row 10: purl
Row 11: (k3, k2tog) 6 times (24)
Row 12: purl
Row 13: (k2, k2tog) 6 times (18)
Row 14: purl
Row 15: (k1, k2tog) 6 times (12)
Row 16: purl
Row 17: (k2tog) 6 times (6)

Break off yarn leaving a long end and transfer to a stitch holder.

BODY

Starting at the base of the body,
cast on 6 st in BLACK

Row 1: (inc-kw) 6 times (12)
Row 2: purl
Row 3: (k1, inc-kw) 6 times (18)
Row 4: purl
Row 5: (k2, inc-kw) 6 times (24)
Row 6-30: continue in stst, starting
and ending with a purl row
Row 31: (k2, k2tog) 6 times (18)
Row 32: purl
Row 33: (k1, k2tog) 6 times (12)
Row 34: purl
Row 35: (k2tog) 6 times (6)

Break off yarn leaving a long end and
transfer stitches to a stitch holder.

ARMS (make 2)

Using 3mm double-ended needles and
leaving a long end, cast on 3 st
using LIME GREEN and work i-cord as
follows

Row 1: k3
Row 2: without turning the work, move
the stitches to the other end of the
needle, pass the wool round the back
of the work. Keeping yarn tight, k3
Row 3-6: repeat row 2

Change to CHARCOAL and Repeat row 2
until the arm measures 85mm.

Break off yarn leaving a long end,
and transfer stitches to a stitch
holder.

LEGS (make 2)

Using 3mm double-ended needles and
leaving a long end, cast on 4 st
using LIME GREEN and work i-cord as
follows

Row 1: k4
Row 2: without turning the work, move
the stitches to the other end of the
needle, pass the wool round the back
of the work. Keeping yarn tight, k4
Repeat row 2 until the leg measures
95mm.

Break off yarn leaving a long end,
and transfer stitches to a stitch
holder

NOSE

Using LIME GREEN and 3mm needles cast
on 8 st

Row 1-3: knit
Row 4: k2tog, k4, k2tog (6)
Row 5: knit
Row 6: k2tog, k2, k2tog (4)
Row 7: knit
Row 8: (k2tog) twice (2)
Row 9: k2tog

Fasten off the yarn leaving an end to
sew nose together.

Skirt

Using BLACK and 3mm needles, cast on
60 st

Rows 1-3: knit
Row 4: purl
Row 5-30: starting with a knit row,
continue in stst

Cast-off kw.

Hat

Using BLACK cast on 26 st

Row 1-4: purl
Row 5-16: continue in stst, starting
with a knit row
Row 17: k1, (k2tog, k1) 8 times, k1 (18)
Row 18: purl
Row 19: (k2tog, k1) 6 times (12)
Row 20: purl
Row 21: (k2tog) 6 times (6)
Row 22: Purl
Row 23: (k2tog) 3 times (3)

Break off yarn leaving a long end,
and transfer stitches to a stitch
holder

Curls (make 10)

Using STEEL and 3mm needles cast on
20 st
Row 1: cast-off tightly kw.

Boots (make 2)

Using BLACK and 4mm needles cast on
14 st

Row 1-2: knit
Row 3: K3, (K2tog) 4 times, K3 (10)
Row 4: K3, (K2tog) twice, K3 (8)
Row 5-6: knit

Cast-off knit-wise.

Break off yarn leaving a long end.

To make up

Head

Fit the safety eyes roughly in the
middle of the head, and close
together. Thread the yarn from the
last row of the head through the
stitches remaining on the needle and
pull tight, then remove the stitches
from the needle.

With right-sides together, sew along
the back of the head, leaving a small
gap at the base for stuffing. Turn
the head the right way out, and stuff
to the required firmness.

Sew together the remaining opening
and feed the end of the yarn back
through the head before cutting off.
Feed the remaining end back through
the head before cutting off.

BODY

Thread the yarn from the last row of the body through the stitches remaining on the needle and pull tight, then remove the stitches from the needle.

With right-sides together, sew along the back of the body, leaving a small gap at the bottom for stuffing. Turn the body the right way out, and stuff to the required firmness.

Sew together the remaining opening and feed the end of the yarn back through the body before cutting off. Feed the remaining end back through the body before cutting off.

ARMS

Thread the yarn from the last row of the arm through the stitches remaining on the needle and pull tight, then remove the stitches from the needle.

Fasten off this end securely. Weave the other loose end up through the arm and cut off the excess.

LEGS

Thread the yarn from the last row of the leg through the stitches remaining on the needle and pull

tight, then remove the stitches from the needle. Fasten off this end securely.

Weave the other loose end up through the leg and cut off the excess.

SKIRT

Bring short ends together to form a loop making sure the work is not twisted and sew along the short edge.

NOSE

Fold the nose in half, and sew together along the edge to form a triangle, leaving the cast-on edge open. Feed the thread back through the nose before trimming.

HAT

Thread the yarn from the last row of the hat through the stitches remaining on the needle and pull tight, then remove the stitches from the needle. With right-sides together, sew along the back of the hat. Feed the remaining end back through the hat before cutting off.

BOOTS

Fold the boot in half and stitch down the back and along the bottom of the boot.

ASSEMBLY:

Attach the head to the body, making sure the eyes point forward (the body seam should be at the back).

Sew the nose to the front of the head between and just below the eyes, adding a little stuffing if desired.

Using the free thread, attach the arms to the body just below the head, one on each side.

Using the free thread, attach the legs to the underside of the body.

Using small running stitch, thread a piece of yarn around the top of the skirt loop, and gather the skirt around the body of the witch, approximately half way down the body. Sew to the body and weave in any loose ends.

Attach the curls to the head, working on alternate sides. Weave in any loose ends. Give the curls a quick twist if they are looking too straight.
Attach the hat to the head, spreading the curls evenly.

Feed each leg into a boot and fasten with a small stitch.

Winter

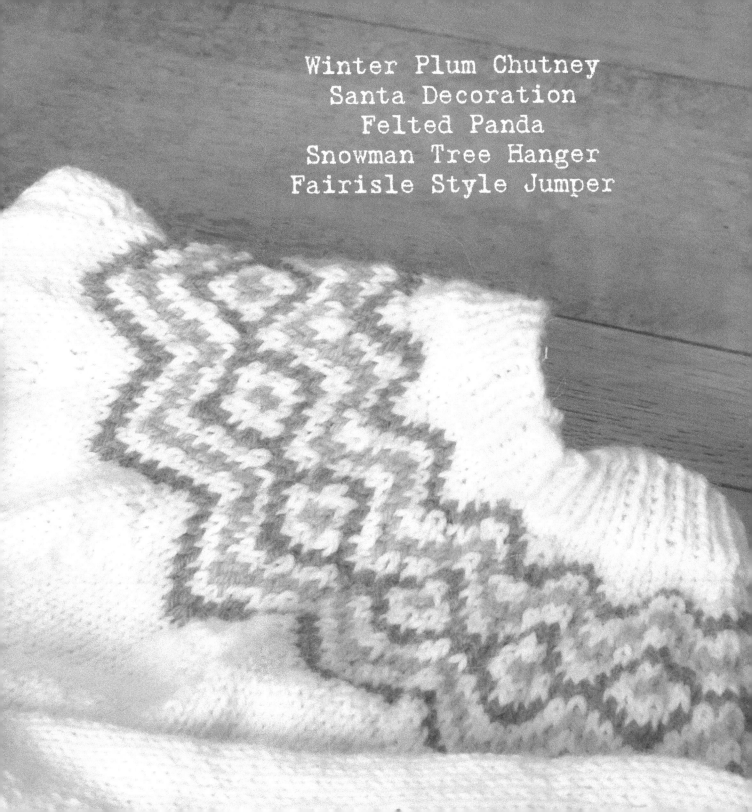

Winter Plum Chutney
Santa Decoration
Felted Panda
Snowman Tree Hanger
Fairisle Style Jumper

Winter Plum Chutney

My nan's pantry was always bursting with preserves and her chutneys were always tasty with cheese. The recipe is so simple and after being left to mature for a while tastes absolutely delicious.

Ingredients:

3 red onions, peeled and chopped into small chunks
1 litre apple cider vinegar
4 large cooking apples. Cored, peeled and chopped
100g plums, pitted with stones removed
400g pears, cored peeled and chopped
2tsp dried garlic
200g dried dates, chopped
300g sultanas
½ tbsp ground allspice
2 tsp ground cinnamon
2 tsp ground ginger
2 tsp ground coriander
1 tsp chilli flakes
1 tbsp salt

1kg soft brown sugar

METHOD:

Before you start making the chutney, you will need to sterilise the jars. A very simple way to do this, is to give them a good wash in hot soapy water. Rinse them well with boiling water, then place on a baking tray. Place the jars in the oven at about 120°C for about 20 mins.

Place the onions in a large saucepan with a little water and cook over a medium-low heat. Once they have softened and become translucent add all the fruit, spices and 500ml of the vinegar. Cook this mixture until the fruit reduces to a pulp, although you want to keep some of the chunks to add a bit of texture to the chutney. Stir occasionally to make sure it doesn't stick to the pan.

Now add the sugar, salt and the remaining vinegar and give the mix a good stir. Keep cooking the mixture until all the sugar has dissolved, and the chutney has started to thicken.

Once the chutney has thickened you can remove it from the heat and pour into the sterilised jars, cover with the lids and allow to cool.

Tip!
This chutney tastes best once it has been allowed to rest for a couple of weeks or so.

SANTA DECORATION

As I lived in Germany as a child, no country does Christmas better
in my opinion. I just love Christmas time. The rich colours, the
Nordic trees and of course Santa.

MATERIALS

Drops Lima DK in black, red, pink &
white
Stuffing
3mm knitting needles
3mm double ended needles
Embroidery needle

MAIN BODY

Using RED and 3mm needles, cast on
10st

Row **1-8:** work in stst starting with a
knit row
Row **9-10:** change to BLACK and work 2
rows in stst starting with a knit row
Row **11-16:** change to RED and work 6
rows in stst starting with a knit row
Row **17:** (k2tog, k2) twice, k2tog (7)
Row **18:** (p1, p2tog) twice, p1 (5)
Row **19:** change to WHITE, (k1, inc-kw)
twice, k1 (7)
Row **20:** (inc-pw, p2) twice, inc-pw
(10)
Row **21:** k2, loop 6, k2
Row **22:** purl
Row **23:** change to PINK, knit
Row **24:** purl
Row **25:** knit
Row **26:** change to WHITE, purl
Row **27:** purl
Row **28:** purl
Row **29:** change to RED, knit
Row **30:** purl

Row 31: (k2tog, k2) twice, k2tog (7)
Row 32: purl
Row 33: (k1, k2tog) twice k1 (5)
Row 34: purl
Row 35: k2tog, k1, k2tog (3)
Row 36: purl
Row 37: k3tog (1)

Break off yarn leaving a long end, and fasten off.

ARMS (make 2)

Using 3mm double pointed needles and RED cast on 2st. Work i-cord as follows:

Row 1: k2
Row 2: without turning the work, move the stitches to the other end of the needle, pass the wool round the back of the work. Keeping yarn tight, k2
Row 3-10: repeat row 2

Break off yarn leaving a long end, and transfer stitches to a stitch holder.

TO MAKE UP

BODY

With right-sides together, sew along the back of the body, leaving a small gap at the bottom for stuffing. Turn the body the right way out, and stuff to the required firmness. Sew together the remaining opening and feed the end of the yarn back through the body before cutting off. Feed the remaining end back through the body before cutting off.

To mark the legs, flatten the body and sew up through the centre for approximately 6 rows.

ARMS

Thread the yarn from the last row of the arm through the stitches remaining on the needle and pull tight, then remove the stitches from the needle. Fasten off this end securely. Weave the other loose end up through the arm and cut off the excess.

FINISHING TOUCHES

Use a small amount of black thread to stitch 2 eyes, and cut the loops to form the beard.

Thread a piece of narrow ribbon or a length of thread through the top of the hat and tie in a knot.

Felted Panda

I had to include my sister's favourite animal, the panda. I did find a childhood picture of me with a panda toy, so I guess I must love them too.

Materials

50g Drops Eskimo in Black
50g Drops Eskimo in White
50g of Drops Lima DK wool in your chosen colour for the scarf
4mm knitting needles
6mm knitting needles
1 pair 6.5mm safety eyes
toy stuffing
darning needle

Body

Using 6mm needles and Drops Eskimo in WHITE, work the standard body from page 119.

With RS together, feed the yarn through the remaining stitches, remove them from the needle and pull tight. Sew along the outer edges of the body, leaving a small opening near the bottom.

Turn the body right side out, and stuff lightly before closing the opening and fastening off the end of the yarn. Feed the remaining end back through the body and cut off the excess.

Head

Using 6mm needles and Drops Eskimo in WHITE, work the standard head from page 119.

Feed the yarn through the remaining stitches, remove them from the needle and pull tight. Fix the safety eyes using the picture as a guide. Bear in mind that the head will shrink during the felting process.

Placing RS together, sew along the outer edges of the head, leaving a small opening near the back of the head.

Turn the head right side out, and stuff lightly before closing the opening and fastening off the end of the yarn. Feed the remaining end back through the head and cut off the excess.

ARMS / LEGS

Using 6mm needles and Drops Eskimo in BLACK, work the standard arms and legs from page 119.

With RS together, feed the yarn through the remaining stitches, remove them from the needle and pull tight. Sew along the outer edges of the arm / leg, leaving a small opening near the bottom.

Turn the arm / leg right side out, and stuff lightly before closing the opening and fastening off the end of the yarn. Feed the remaining end back through the arm / leg and cut off the excess.

EARS (make 2)

Using 6mm needles and Drops Eskimo in BLACK, cast on 2st.

Row 1: (inc-kw) twice (4)
Row 2-5: knit
Row 6: (k2tog) twice (2)

Break off yarn leaving an end and transfer stitches to a stitch holder. Attach the ears to the sides of the head, using the picture as a guide.

FELTING

Now it is time for the felting process. For detailed instructions of the method I use, refer to page 122. Sometimes you can be left with small holes in the felted surface, where the stuffing can poke through. If these are not too large, they can either be darned, or alternatively you could cover them by sewing a small patch of colourful fabric over the opening. Sometimes though there is no option but to re-make the piece.

Once you are happy all the pieces have felted correctly, you can proceed to assemble the bear. Attach the head, arms and legs to the body using a strong cotton. I like to use quilting thread as it is extremely strong. Be careful when pulling it tight though - I have been known to cut myself with the thread! I also like to use a doll needle. These are essentially very long needles, and make reaching under the head much easier. If you don't have these then a normal sewing needle will do.

Using some black embroidery thread, sew the nose and mouth as described on page 124.

THE SCARF.

Using 4mm needles and your chosen colour of drops Lima, cast on 8 st.

Row 1-4: knit
Row 5-40: work in stst starting with a knit row
Row 41-44: knit

Cast-off knit wise and sew in loose ends.

Fold the scarf around the neck of the panda and fasten with a button.

Snowman Tree Hanger

Christmas wouldn't be Christmas without a snowman, so here he is with his little white body, his carrot nose and little scarf to keep him warm.

Materials.

DK wool in white, black, orange and your chosen scarf colour
stuffing
3mm knitting needles
3mm double ended needles
embroidery needle

Body

Using 3mm needles and WHITE cast on 7 st

Row 1: (k1, inc-kw) 3 times, k1 (10)
Row 2: purl
Row 3: (k1, inc-kw, inc-kw) 3 times, k1 (16)
Row 4: purl
Row 5: k1, (inc-kw, k2) 5 times (21)
Row 6: purl
Row 7: knit
Row 8: purl
Row 9: k1, (k2tog, k2) 5 times (16)
Row 10: purl
Row 11: (k1, k2tog, k2tog) 3 times, k1 (10)
Row 12: purl
Row 13: (k1, k2tog) 3 times, k1 (7)
Row 14: purl
Row 15: (k1, inc-kw) 3 times, k1 (10)
Row 16: purl
Row 17: (k1, inc-kw, inc-kw) 3 times, k1 (16)
Row 18: purl
Row 19: (k1, k2tog, k2tog) 3 times, k1 (10)
Row 20: purl
Row 21: (k1, k2tog) 3 times, k1 (7)
Row 22: (p1, p2tog) twice, p1 (5)

Row 23: (k1, inc-kw) twice, k1 (7)
Row 24: (inc-pw, p2) twice, inc-pw (10)
Row 25: knit
Row 26: purl
Row 27: knit
Row 28: purl
Row 29: change to BLACK, knit
Row 30: purl
Row 31: knit
Row 32: purl
Row 33: (k2tog, k2) twice, k2tog (7)
Row 34: purl
Row 35: (k1, k2tog) twice, k1 (5)
Row 36: purl
Row 37: k2tog, k1, k2tog (3)
Row 38: purl
Row 39: k3tog (1)

Break off yarn and fasten off.

ARMS (make 2)

Using 3mm double pointed needles and WHITE cast on 2st. Work I cord as follows:

Row 1: k2
Row 2: without turning the work, move the stitches to the other end of the needle, pass the wool round the back of the work. Keeping yarn tight, k2
Row 3-10: repeat row 2

Break off yarn leaving a long end, and transfer stitches to a stitch holder.

NOSE

Using 3mm double pointed needles and ORANGE cast on 3st. Work i-cord as follows:

Row 1: k3
Row 2: without turning the work, move the stitches to the other end of the needle, pass the wool round the back of the work. Keeping yarn tight, k3
Row 3: repeat row 2

Break off yarn leaving a long end, and transfer stitches to a stitch holder.

SCARF

Using 3mm needles and your chosen colour cast on 25st

Rows 1-3: knit

Cast off.

TO MAKE UP

BODY

With right-sides together, sew along the back of the body, leaving a small gap at the bottom for stuffing. Turn the body the right way out, and stuff to the required firmness. Sew together the remaining opening and feed the end of the yarn back through the body before cutting off. Feed the remaining end back through the body before cutting off.

ARMS

Thread the yarn from the last row of the arm through the stitches remaining on the needle and pull tight, then remove the stitches from the needle. Fasten off this end securely. Weave the other loose end up through the arm and cut off the excess.

NOSE

Thread the yarn from the last row of the nose through the stitches remaining on the needle and pull tight, then remove the stitches from the needle. Fasten off this end securely. Weave the other loose end up through the nose and cut off the excess.

SCARF

Sew in the loose ends.

ASSEMBLY:

Sew the nose to the front of the head, roughly in the centre.

Using the free thread, attach the arms to the body just below the head, one on each side.

Using some black yarn, make 2 small eyes using small stitches.

Using some black or orange thread, make 3 buttons using simple stitches.

Wrap the scarf around his neck.

Thread a piece of narrow ribbon or a length of thread through the top of the hat and tie in a knot.

FAIRISLE STYLE JUMPER

My mother told me she knitted a jumper once as a gift. It was a labour of love and took her a long time to finish. This simple child's jumper is knitted in the round. It knits up quickly and will be an impressive gift for family or friends.

MATERIALS:

200g Drops Lima DK in white
50g Drops Lima DK in grey
50g Drops Lima DK in yellow
4mm circular needle
4mm double ended needles
embroidery needle.

Gauge: 22st and 31 rows to 10cm in stst.

Finished size: 60cm around chest, 38cm from neck to bottom edge, 23cm from underarm to end of sleeve.

PATTERN:

Using 4mm circular needle and main colour A, cast on 79 stitches. Join into a round by passing the last stitch from the right-hand needle to the left-hand needle, making sure you have not twisted the cast-on stitches, then k2tog. (78 st). Place a stitch marker on the right-hand needle to mark the start of the round.

Neck rib: (k1, p1) to end of round. Repeat this row until the rib measures 3cm.

YOKE:

Row 1-3: knit
Rows 4-29: work pattern block as shown on page 98 a total of 13 times on each row, increasing where indicated (rows 5, 10 & 18). At this point you should have 156st.
Row 30: (inc-kw, k10, inc-kw) 13 times (182)
Rows 31-33: knit
Row 34: (inc-kw, k12, inc-kw) 13 times (208)

Rows 35-43: knit

Row 44: k25, inc-kw, (k51, inc-kw) 3 times, k26 (212)

Row 45: k31, pass the next 44 st to a stitch holder. Turn the work and cast on 6 st. Turn the work and k62, pass the next 44 st onto a stitch holder, turn the work and cast on 6 st, turn the work and k31.

You should now have 136 on the circular needle and two sets of 44 st on stitch holders.

BODY:

Continue knitting on the main 136 st until the piece measures 20cm from the underarm cast-on stitches, making sure you finish the round at the stitch marker.

Bottom rib: (k1, p1) to end of round. Repeat this row until the rib measures 3cm.

Cast off in rib.

SLEEVES - work 2 the same.

Pass the 44 st from one of the stitch holders evenly onto 4mm double pointed needles. At the underarm section, using main colour A, pick up 3st, place a marker, then pick up another 3st. (50 st).

Using the stitch marker as the start of a round, work on these 50 st until the sleeve measures 2cm from the underarm.

Next row: k2tog, k46, k2tog (48 st) - note the decreases should be either side of the stitch marker.

Continue knitting, repeating the decrease either side of the stitch marker every 4.5cm until you have 40st remaining.

Continue on these 40st until the sleeve measures 21cm overall from the underarm.

Wrist rib: (k1, p1) to end. (k1, p1) to end of round. Repeat this row until the rib measures 3cm.

Cast off in rib.
To finish the sweater, sew in all loose ends.

Colour chart

● Yellow

■ Grey

○ inc-kw

Tip!
When reading a colout chart, start from the bottom right square and work towards the top left. The pattern will tell you how many times to repease the chart.

Useful information

KNITTING ABBREVIATIONS

Here is a full list of all the knitting abbreviations I have used throughout this book.

k: knit
p: purl
inc-kw: increase knit-wise by knitting into the front and back of the same stitch
inc-pw: increase purl-wise by purling into the front and back of the same stitch
k2tog: knit 2 together
p2tog: purl 2 together
skpo: slip the next stitch, k1, pass the slip stitch over the stitch you just knitted
st: stitch
stst: stocking stitch - work alternate rows of knit and purl
(n): n number of stitches
(xxx) n times: repeat (xxx) n number of times

GENERAL TERMS:

(n): n number of stitches
(xxx) n times: repeat (xxx) n number of times
RW: right sides
WS: wrong sides

CROCHET ABBREVIATIONS

Here is a full list of crochet abbreviations I have used in this book. Note all my patterns are based on **UK** terms, but I have included a comparison between UK & US.

<u>UK (USED IN THIS BOOK)</u>	<u>US</u>

ss - slip stitch
ch - chain
dc - double crochet   **sc** - single crochet
htr - half treble crochet   **hdc** - half double crochet
tr - treble crochet   **dc** - double crochet
dtr - double treble crochet   **tr** - triple crochet
ttr - triple treble crochet   **dtc** - double triple crochet
dc2tog - double crochet 2 stitches   **sc2tog** - single crochet 2 stitches
together   together
dtr3tog - work 3 double treble   **tr3tog** - triple crochet 3 stitches
crochet stitches together   together

<u>GENERAL TERMS:</u>

(n): n number of stitches
(xxx) n times: repeat (xxx) n number of times
RW: right sides
WS: wrong sides

KEY FOR CROCHET STITCH CHARTS (UK TERMS)

- • slip st (ss)
- ◦ chain (ch)
- ✛ double crochet (dc)

⊤ half treble (htr)

⊤ treble (tr)

⧊ double treble (htr)

⧊ tripple treble (tr)

Sewing animal noses

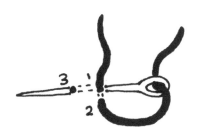

1. Start by positioning pins in the places indicated by the dots to set the size and position of the nose and mouth.

2. Start by inserting the needle at point 1 which will be midway between 2 of the pins, then coming out at point 2. Go back in at point 1, then out at point 3.

3. Now go back in at point 4, then out at point 5. Repeat this stage working down to the point of the nose.

4. To start the mouth, go in at point 6, then out at point 7. Repeat a couple of times.

5. To form the left side of the mouth, go in at point 8, then out at point 9. Again repeat a couple of times.

6. To form the right side, go in at point 10, then out at point 11. Again repeat a couple of times.

7. To finish, go in at point 12 where the two sides of the mouth meet, then out at point 13. Now go back in just below point 13, and back out near the top of the nose. Carefully cut the ends as close as possible to the face.

FELTED ANIMALS - BASIC FORM

This basic form is the starting point for all the felted animals in this book.

BODY

Starting at the base of the body cast on 6 st

Row 1: inc-kw 6 times (12)
Row 2: purl
Row 3: (k1, inc-kw) 6 times (18)
Row 4: purl
Row 5: (k2, inc-kw) 6 times (24)
Row 6: purl
Row 7: k10, inc-kw, k2, inc-kw, k10 (26)
Row 8: p10, inc-pw, p1, inc-pw twice, p1, inc-pw, p10 (30)
Row 9: k10, inc-kw, k1, inc-kw, k4, inc-kw, k1, inc-kw, k10 (34)
Row 10: purl
Row 11: knit
Row 12: purl
Row 13: k10, k2tog, k1, k2tog, k4, k2tog, k1, k2tog, k10 (30)
Row 14: p10, p2tog, p1, p2tog twice, p1, p2tog, p10 (26)
Row 15: k10, k2tog, k2, k2tog, k10 (24)
Row 16-24: starting and ending with a purl row, continue in stst
Row 25: (k2, k2tog) 6 times (18)
Row 26: purl
Row 27: (k1, k2tog) 6 times (12)
Row 28: purl
Row 29: k2tog 6 times (6)

Break off yarn leaving a long end to sew up body, and transfer stitches to a stitch holder.

ARMS / LEGS (MAKE 4)

Starting at the top of the arm cast on 4 st

Row 1: inc-kw 4 times (8)
Row 2: purl
Row 3-22: continue in stst

Break off yarn leaving a long end to sew up arm, and transfer stitches to a stitch holder.

HEAD

Starting at the nose and leaving a long end, cast on 3 st
Row 1: inc-kw 3 times (6)
Row 2: purl
Row 3: inc-kw 6 times (12)
Row 4: purl
Row 5-8: continue in stst
Row 9: (inc-kw, k2, inc-kw) 3 times (18)
Row 10: purl

Row 11: k5, inc-kw, k6, inc-kw, k5 (20)
Row 12: purl
Row 13: k6, inc-kw, k6, inc-kw, k6 (22)
Row 14: purl
Row 15: k7, inc-kw, k6, inc-kw, k7 (24)
Row 16: purl
Row 17: k8, inc-kw, k6, inc-kw, k8 (26)
Row 18: purl
Row 19: k9, inc-kw, k6, inc-kw, k9 (28)
Row 20: purl
Row 21: k9, k2tog, k6, k2tog, k9 (26)
Row 22: p8 p2tog, p6, p2tog, p8 (24)
Row 23: k7, k2tog, k6, k2tog, k7 (22)
Row 24: purl
Row 25: (k2tog) 11 times (11)
Row 26: (p2tog) twice, p3, (p2tog) twice (7)

Break yarn leaving a long end for sewing up the head, and place the stitches on a stitch holder.

THE FELTING PROCESS.

Hot felting, as the name suggests, is basically the process of producing felt from woollen items using the addition of heat. The process itself is very straightforward and can be done in a few ways. The methods I use are hand felting and machine felting, and I will describe both here.

When you are felting, you are agitating the fibres in the wool and causing them to bind together - the opposite of what you do when you create yarn. Using heat helps speed the process up as well as causing the fibres to shrink, forming a tighter finish. It is important to note that this works best with natural fibres rather than synthetic.

The type of yarn you use is also important. All wools will felt to different degrees, for instance sheep's wool may felt better than Alpaca, but avoid anything marked as 'superwashed' as this is wool that has been specially processed to make it machine washable, and will not felt (normally).

MATERIALS:

So, the materials you need for hot felting are:

A woollen article - could be knitted or crocheted
Soap - note this is important as it helps open up the fibres. Normal washing detergent will be far less effective.
Hot water - the hotter the better, but not so hot as to scald yourself if hand felting!

MACHINE FELTING - my favourite as you don't have to do much!

Machine felting is basically carried out in the washing machine. It is much easier as you don't have to put much effort in, but it can be a bit hit and miss as all machines wash things slightly differently.

There a few things to note when felting in the washing machine, not least of which is that during the process the items will give off a lot of fibres, so you may want to put the items to be felted in a bag such as pillowcase just in case.

Put a small amount of liquid soap or soap flakes in the detergent draw. Note it is important to use soap rather than normal washing detergent as it opens up the fibres of the wool.

When felting in the washing machine, you need to set the temperature to 60°C as a minimum and choose a fairly long cycle to ensure there is plenty of agitation of the items. Start the wash cycle and wait.

When the cycle has finished, remove the items from the machine and press with a towel to remove excess water. If the items have not felted as much as you would like and the stitches are still very visible, then simply but back through the wash. When you are happy with the result, allow the items to dry naturally.

HAND FELTING

Hand felting can be very rewarding as you see the felting take place before your eyes.

Part fill a large bowl with water which is as hot as you can stand to put your hands in. The hotter the better, but not so hot as to scald yourself. Add a small amount of soap to the water and mix well. If using soap flakes, make sure they are properly dissolved.

Place the first item to be felted in the water and allow to sit for a couple of minutes. Now this is where the hard work comes in. For the felting process to work, you need to rub the item to cause the fibres to start to fix together. Don't be alarmed if you don't see anything happening straight away, it can take a few minutes before you start to see any difference.

Keep checking the item you are felting regularly, and once you are happy with the result, rinse in cold water, then remove excess water with a towel, pull back into shape and allow to dry naturally.

LOOP STITCH

1. Start to knit the stitch as normal, but stop before you slip the stitch off the needle.

2. Bring the wool forward between the needles, round your left thumb, then back between the needles.

3. Pass the first loop of the stitch from the right needle to the left.

4. Knit BOTH loops of the stitch together by pushing the right needle through the loops from left to right.

5. Wrap the wool round the right needle then finish knitting the stitch.

6. As you slip the stitch off the needle pull the loop tight to secure it.

If you are having trouble following these instructions, there are plenty of videos available on the internet to show you several methods to produce a loop stitch.

3 NEEDLE CAST-OFF

1. Place the two pieces with RS facing. Using a third needle, pass it through the FRONT of the first stitch on the other two needles.

2. Wrap the yarn around the third needle as you would for a normal knit stitch.

3. Pull the yarn back through both stitches to form the new stitch.

4. Slip the stitch off the other two needles as you would for a knit stitch.

5. Repeat steps 1 to 4 with the next stitch.

6. To form the cast-off, slip the first stitch on the right needle, over the second as you would for a normal cast-off.

7. When finished, the cast-off will leave a small ridge on the WS of the work. If you would like to make a feature of this ridge, then starting with the WS together will form a ridge on the RS of the work.

Suppliers

Here is a list of suppliers I used to source the materials for use in this book. I hope you find the list useful. They are all based in the UK but they also do mail order.

Wool Warehouse
12 Longfield Road
Sydenham Industrial Estate
Leamington Spa
Warwickshire
CV31 1XB
www.woolwarehouse.co.uk

TOFT UK
Toft Studio,
Toft Lane
Dunchurch
Warwickshire
CV22 6NR
www.toftuk.com

Acknowledgements

I have really enjoyed putting this book together, and I hope you enjoy making the projects. Although it may be my name on the front of the book, it wouldn't have come together without the help of a lot of people behind the scenes.

A huge thank you to my family who have had to put up with me shouting when I have dropped stitches or run out of wool, and of course test my recipes which didn't always go to plan first time round. Somehow, they keep supporting me, as does my mum.

Two special ladies, Amanda Keech and Lesley Brown who have kindly tested my crochet and knitting patterns for me. I can't thank them enough

And a final thank you to Katie McCullough for the fabulous family photo opposite. You can find more of her fabulous work on her website: www.katiemcculloughphotography.co.uk

Other Books by Kerry Lucas

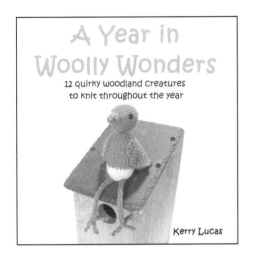

A Year in Woolly Wonders - 12 quirky woodland creatures to knit throughout the year.

ISBN: 978-1-9997429-04

'this book is perfect with a different animal to craft for each month' - Let's Knit magazine

'Packed with 12 woodland animal knits, it really is a bookshelf gem' - Simply Knitting magazine

A Woollyful Christmas

ISBN: 978-1-9997429-11

Have yourself a Woollyful Christmas with this collection of fun festive knits.

Building on the success of her first book 'A Year in Woolly Wonders', Kerry has designed a wonderful group of festive friends to adorn your home or tree at Christmas.

Lightning Source UK Ltd.
Milton Keynes UK
UKHW021023240322
400542UK00005B/79